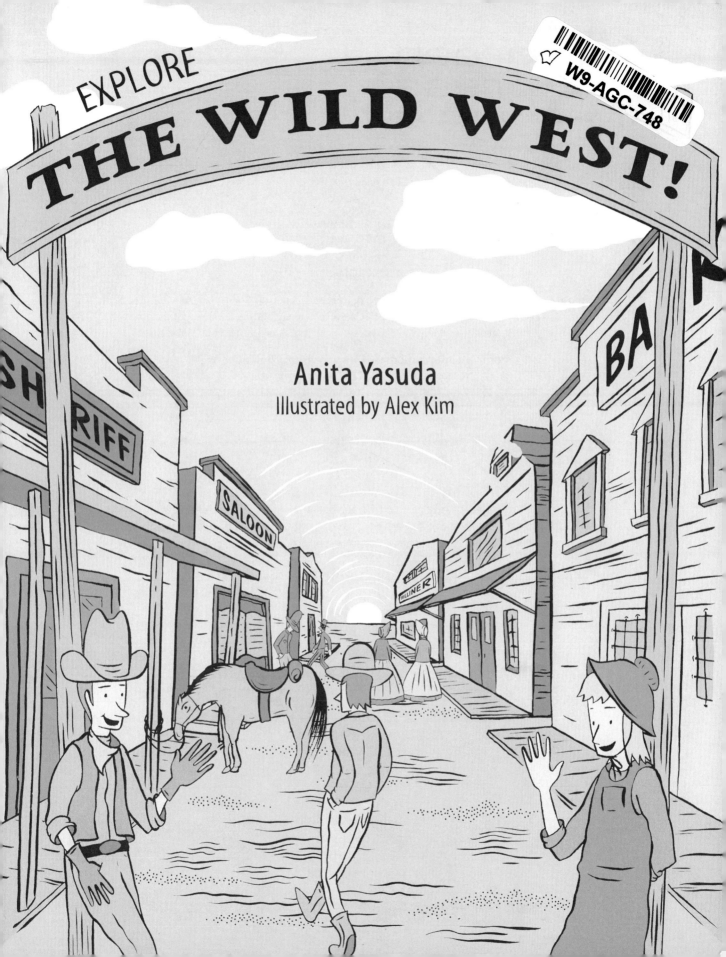

green press INITIATIVE

Nomad Press is committed to preserving ancient forests and natural resources.
We elected to print *Explore the Wild West!* on 30% post consumer recycled paper,
processed chlorine free. As a result, for this printing, we have saved:

10 Trees (40' tall and 6-8" diameter)
4,526 Gallons of Wastewater
4 million BTU's of Total Energy
286 Pounds of Solid Waste
1,004 Pounds of Greenhouse Gases

Nomad Press made this paper choice because our printer, Thomson-Shore, Inc., is a member of
Green Press Initiative, a nonprofit program dedicated to supporting authors, publishers,
and suppliers in their efforts to reduce their use of fiber obtained from endangered forests.

For more information, visit www.greenpressinitiative.org

This book was manufactured by Thomson-Shore, Inc.,
Dexter, Michigan, USA
July 2012, Job #582447
ISBN: 978-1-936749-71-3

Illustrations by Alex Kim
Educational Consultant, Marla Conn

Questions regarding the ordering of this book should be addressed to
Independent Publishers Group
814 N. Franklin St.
Chicago, IL 60610
www.ipgbook.com

Nomad Press
2456 Christian St.
White River Junction, VT 05001
www.nomadpress.net

FSC® C013483 MIX Paper from responsible sources

Manufactured by Thomson-Shore, Dexter, MI (USA); RMA582HS447, July, 2012

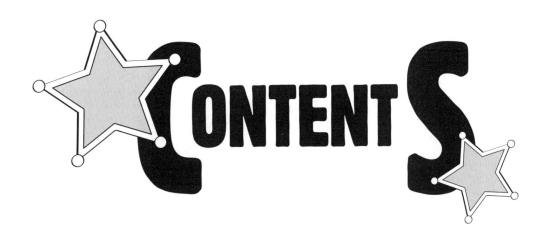

CONTENTS

Introduction
Let's Explore the
Wild West! ~ 1

Chapter One
Where Was the
Wild West? ~ 3

Chapter Two
Gold Rush Miners ~ 10

Chapter Three
Moving West ~ 24

Chapter Four
Pioneer Life ~ 39

Chapter Five
Frontier Towns and
Lawmen ~ 50

Chapter Six
Native People in
the West ~ 62

Chapter Seven
Cowboys ~ 75

Glossary ⋆⋆⋆ **Resources** ⋆⋆⋆ **Index**

Titles in the **Explore Your World!** Series

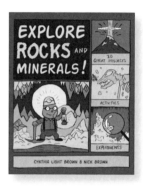

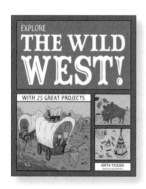

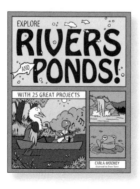

Let's Explore the Wild West!

Have you ever gone on a road trip? You probably brought lots of games. And if you ran out of food, you could stop at a restaurant. But in the early and mid-1800s, none of this was possible. Going west meant moving there—and selling your home and most of your things first. Your remaining belongings, plus food and supplies, were piled into a wagon 10 feet long and 4 feet wide (3 meters long and 1 meter wide). What would your parents say if you asked them, "Are we there yet?" You might not have been very happy to hear, "Not for five months or so."

EXPLORE THE WILD WEST!

What was the Wild West? Where was it? What was it like to live in America over 150 years ago? What did kids and their parents who headed west wear, eat, and do for fun? In this book you'll explore the Wild West, and an exciting time of discovery and **settlement** during the 1800s.

WORDS to KNOW!

settlement: a new community where people have not lived before.

Explore the Wild West! will answer many of your questions. It will introduce you to some amazing people along the way, like James Beckwourth, William Frederick Cody, and Sitting Bull. There will be lots of silly jokes, and fun facts, too. Don't be surprised if by the end of this book you start singing saddle songs, cooking trail food, and making your own covered wagon.

What are you waiting for partner? Put on your boots and lower your hat. Let's explore the Wild West!

Where Was the Wild West?

The "Wild West" was more than just a place. It was more than the western lands beyond the Mississippi River. It was a time of **pioneers**, **cowboys**, and **Native Americans**. It was a time of cowgirls and pioneer women, stagecoaches, saloons, outlaws and lawmen, buffalo hunting, and bank robbers.

WORDS  KNOW!

pioneer: one of the first to settle in a new land.

cowboy: a person who works on horseback to care for cattle.

Native Americans: the people already living in America before new settlers arrived.

EXPLORE THE WILD WEST!

WORDS ★ to ★ KNOW!

frontier: the edge of what is settled.

What we think of as the time of the Wild West started in the early 1800s. By the mid-1800s, when gold was discovered in California, everyone was talking about the Wild West. This period of time lasted until the **frontier** was closed in 1890.

The original American frontier was the Mississippi River. But the frontier pushed west towards the Pacific Ocean as tens of thousands of people moved westward. Stories of plenty of good farmland for everyone made the West sound amazing. Many pioneers went to Oregon and other places because the land was free. When gold was discovered, more and more people moved there, hoping to strike it rich.

How America Grew

How did America get new land for people to explore and settle? In 1803, the United States doubled its size with a single purchase of land—the **Louisiana Purchase**. The leader of France, Napoleon Bonaparte, sold the Louisiana Territory to President Thomas Jefferson. This area included parts or all of the present-day states of Louisiana, Missouri, Arkansas, Texas, Iowa, Minnesota, Kansas, Nebraska, Colorado, North Dakota, South Dakota, Montana, Wyoming, Oklahoma, and New Mexico.

WORDS to KNOW!

Louisiana Purchase: the land west of the Mississippi River bought from France in 1803.

water route: a way to get somewhere over rivers and lakes.

continent: one of the earth's major land masses.

Now that America reached far to the west, President Jefferson needed a map of the area. He sent two men, named Meriwether Lewis and William Clark, to do the job. He hoped they would discover a **water route** across the **continent**. Lewis and Clark and their 50-person team explored the West from 1804 to 1806, becoming the first new Americans to see the Pacific Ocean.

THEN: The American government paid France $15 million for the Louisiana Territory.

NOW: Today, this land deal would cost billions of dollars.

WORDS KNOW!

trapper: someone who traps animals for food or their skins.

missionary: a person sent to convert Native Americans to the Christian religion.

Oregon Trail: a route to Oregon that was very close to Lewis and Clark's route.

pelt: an animal skin.

A French Canadian **trapper** and his Native American wife, Sacagawea, translated for Lewis and Clark. This allowed them to speak to the Native Americans they met along the way. When Native American people saw Sacagawea, they believed the group was peaceful.

Lewis and Clark kept detailed journals of the plants and animals they discovered. They wrote about the Native Americans they met. Along the way, they sent boxes of seeds, bones, animal skins—and even a live prairie dog—back to President Jefferson.

After Lewis and Clark's successful two-year expedition, many explorers, scientists, map makers, and **missionaries** headed west on the **Oregon Trail**. Fur traders, often called mountain men, went west along the Oregon Trail too. These men trapped beaver and other small animals. They also traded many goods with Native Americans, such as rifles and steel knives for more beaver **pelts**. Mountain men used their knowledge of the land to guide soldiers and explorers.

Did You Know?

Lewis and Clark's journey still has an effect on our lives today. Many of their routes are used for railways and highways. Their plant specimens are studied by scientists. We even use some of Lewis and Clark's place names, like Camp Fortunate in Montana.

Presenting . . . James Beckwourth

Born in 1798, James Beckwourth was a famous African American mountain man. He worked as a fur trapper, guide, and translator. He lived among the Crow Indians where he learned to speak their language. Around 1850, Beckwourth discovered a trail through the Sierra Nevada Mountains that was good enough for wagons. Many settlers and gold miners travelling to California used his route. The Beckwourth Pass is named for him.

The trails and **posts** used by these explorers and mountain men guided the pioneers who came to settle the land west of the Mississippi River. Men, women, and children heading west walked, pushed **handcarts**, and rode on horses and in wagons. Few knew how hard and long the journey would be.

WORDS to KNOW!

post: a fort providing supplies to settlers on the trails and to fur traders.

handcart: a small wooden cart pushed by hand.

FRONTIER Quick Quote

". . . those who will come after us will extend . . . and fill up the canvas we begin." —**Thomas Jefferson, 1805**

Quick Quote Translation: President Jefferson believed people in the future would explore and settle in the West, where Lewis and Clark had first explored.

MAP YOUR OWN
Lewis and Clark's Route

President Thomas Jefferson hoped Lewis and Clark would find a water route to the Pacific Ocean. People and goods could travel across the country by water more easily than by land. It would open up new trading opportunities, as well. **Have an adult supervise while you are on the Internet.**

1 Use Lewis and Clark's journal entries and map as a reference. Go to www.loc.gov/teachers/classroommaterials/ presentationsandactivities/presentations/lewisandclark/

2 To print out a map of the United States, go to www.nomadpress.net/resources.

3 First, label the Atlantic and Pacific Oceans. Then draw stars at the following three locations: St. Louis, Missouri, the beginning of Lewis and Clark's journey; Fort Mandan, where the team wintered in 1804; and Clatsop, Oregon, the end of Lewis and Clark's trail.

4 Find the Missouri, Mississippi, and Columbia Rivers and trace them in blue. Label the Rocky Mountains.

5 Mark Lewis and Clark's route with a black pencil. Label the states that Lewis and Clark's expedition passed through. How many miles do you think they traveled?

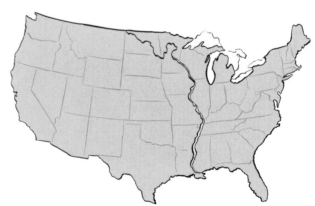

MAKE YOUR OWN
Jefferson Peace Medal

Lewis and Clark took 89 peace medals with them. They gave the medals to Native Americans as a symbol of friendship between the American government and the native people. One side of the medal showed a silhouette of President Jefferson. The opposite side showed two hands clasped together, a tomahawk, a peace pipe, and the words Peace and Friendship. Native Americans often decorated their medals with traditional feathers or beads. You can make one too.

SUPPLIES

drinking glass
sheet of paper
pencil
scissors
fine tip colored markers
large safety pin
assorted small beads
that can fit on the pin
crafting feathers
clear tape

1 Place the drinking glass on the paper and trace around it.

2 Use the pencil to sketch designs within the circle. You could include hands, words, and symbols.

3 Cut out your medal with the scissors and decorate it with glitter and markers.

4 Carefully poke the safety pin through the top of your medal. Thread beads through the safety pin and tape on feathers.

5 You can give your medal to a friend and make more to share.

Gold Rush Miners

In 1848 in California, a carpenter named John Marshall noticed some shiny rocks in the American River. They weren't just any rocks—they were gold nuggets! John and his fellow workers at the sawmill didn't want the news to get out. They hoped to keep the gold to themselves. But their secret didn't stay quiet for long.

Sam Brannan, owner of *The Star* newspaper, went to San Francisco with a bottle of gold dust. "Gold!" he shouted in the streets. "Gold from the American River." This sparked gold madness. But Sam was clever. Before his announcement, Sam had bought all the mining supplies miners would need to dig for gold. And then he made a fortune selling them!

Just how crazy did "gold fever" get? Two newspapers in San Francisco shut their doors when most of their readers and staff left for the gold fields. Even public schools were ordered closed!

Did You Know?

So many gold hunters left for California in 1849 that people began calling them the '49ers.

WORDS ★ to ★ KNOW!

wagon train: a group of pioneers travelling across the country together by wagon.

Presenting . . . Rufus Porter

With so many people rushing to get to California, businessmen started selling seats on **wagon trains** and mules. In 1849, one clever inventor named Rufus Porter designed a flying machine powered by steam engines to fly pioneers west! It would float in the sky using a large, gas-filled tube. Porter claimed he could take 50 to 100 people from New York to California in only three days. Unfortunately, his flying machine never took off!

Farmers, soldiers, and businessmen poured into California to stake their **claims**. Miners from practically every continent came too. From 1849 to 1850, California's population went from 14,000 to 100,000. By 1850, there were 500 **abandoned** ships in San Francisco harbor, left stranded by their crews!

Everyone wanted the chance to get rich quick. Stories spread of being able to make 10 times more money in California than back East. Sadly, many miners found nothing and some didn't even have enough money to get back home.

WORDS ★ to ★ KNOW!

claim: a parcel of land 50 to 100 feet wide (15 to 30 meters). A miner arriving there first could claim a right to search there for gold or other metals.

abandon: to leave behind.

Ho! For California

People went by ship, wagon, horseback, or on foot to reach California. They stocked up with supplies such as tents, kettles, ropes, lanterns, rifles, and food in towns along the Missouri River. With these "California fixings," they set out for months in the wilderness, to face extreme heat, cold, and disease.

Did You Know?

Along the way, miners changed the words of the song "Oh Susanna!" to "Oh, California! That's the land for me; I'm going to Sacramento; With my washbowl on my knee."

Those who could afford it went to California by sea on a **clipper ship**. They quickly realized that advertisements describing "magnificent and fast sailing ships" did not give the full picture. The most direct way to sail to San Francisco Bay was 15,000 miles long (24,140 kilometers), and took nearly five months. It included a trip around **Cape Horn**! Passengers faced the dangers of the sea, disease, and rotten food.

WORDS to KNOW!

clipper ship: a fast sailing ship with three masts and square sails.

Cape Horn: the southernmost tip of South America.

Isthmus of Panama: a narrow strip of land between the Caribbean Sea and the Pacific Ocean in Central America.

malaria: a disease spread by infected mosquitoes. It is found mainly in the hot areas near the equator.

Some miners got off in Panama and traveled over the **Isthmus of Panama** to the Pacific side. They hoped it would be quicker than going all the way around South America. Many caught diseases like **malaria** and died before ever boarding another ship to take them north to California.

Life in a Tent Town

In California, the '49ers set up camps near mining sites. These became known as "tent towns." Some had colorful names like Gouge Eye, Poor Man's Creek, and Mad Mule Gulch. The towns were not much more than a sea of canvas shelters.

Men were charged high prices for supplies there. Pans that cost a few cents before the gold rush now went for $10. Even breakfast cost 10 times what it did back East. One miner reported paying $500 for four bushels of apples shipped from Oregon to the gold mines. That's about $3 a pound, which is expensive for apples even today!

If a miner did get lucky and find gold, he celebrated with a Hangtown Fry of fried oysters, eggs, and bacon. It sure beat the usual meal of beans.

THEN & NOW

THEN: Miners getting off a ship in Panama had to cross a narrow strip of land known as the Isthmus of Panama to reach the Pacific Ocean.

NOW: Ships today use the Panama Canal. It was built between 1904 and 1914 to make a water route between the Atlantic and Pacific Oceans.

Early on, there were only a few women and children in the mining towns. Some women worked as cooks. Lucy Stoddard Wakefield was one woman who made her money cooking for miners. She baked 240 pies a week for $1 a pie. Women could also make $10 a day sewing overalls for the miners. This was more money than many miners ever made.

WORDS ★ to ★ KNOW!

denim: a sturdy cotton twill fabric, typically blue, used for jeans, overalls, and other clothing.

So, who did make it rich in the gold fields? Some people made fortunes selling goods to the miners. Levi Strauss arrived in California in 1850 to make clothes for miners. He made pants from tent canvas and ships' sails. Then he got his hands on **denim** and made his fortune in blue jeans. That means the "Levi" jeans people wear today can be traced all the way back to the Gold Rush!

Did You Know?

Miners often spoke of "seeing the elephant." Pioneers on the Oregon Trail said it too. It wasn't a real elephant but a symbol of the ups and downs of a miner's search for gold or a pioneer's hard time on the trail. The expression was based on an old story about a farmer who had a lot of bad luck on his way to a circus. The farmer said that he didn't care as he had "seen an elephant."

Gold Hunting Tools

Gathering gold took patience and hard work. In the beginning, miners found gold easily in streams and riverbeds. They used a shallow pan to scoop up water and dirt. They carefully swirled the pan around, letting the dirt wash out. The gold, a heavier mineral, was left behind. Not every piece was a good-sized nugget. Most were no larger than the head of a pin.

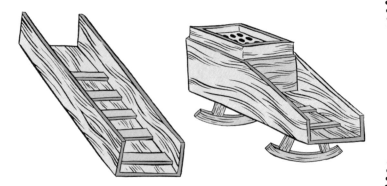

Later, hand-panning was replaced by equipment like **sluice boxes** or **cradles**. A wooden sluice box looked like a steep ramp. As water ran down the ramp, gold was caught in wooden strips at the bottom. Cradles were also made of wood but had a strainer inside to sift the gold from the dirt. Miners rocked it back and forth in the water until the gold collected in the bottom.

WORDS to KNOW!

sluice box: a long box used to separate gold from dirt.

cradle: a wooden box used to sift for gold.

discrimination: the unfair treatment of a person or a group of people because of who they are.

famine: a severe shortage of food.

Foreign Miners Tax: an 1852 tax of $3 a month charged to Chinese miners.

foreign: from another country.

ban: to prevent by law.

immigrate: to come to a new country to live there permanently.

Minority Miners

During the Gold Rush, only 1 percent of the population was African American. Most African American gold miners had been slaves. Some used their gold finds to buy freedom for their families.

As gold became harder to find, violence against miners from other countries increased. Those from Mexico, Chile, and China were targeted. The Chinese faced some of the worst **discrimination**.

Thousands of Chinese men came to California to find gold. There was widespread **famine** in China at the time. This was a chance for men to provide food for their families. They had learned of the gold discovery from trade ships at Chinese ports. Unfortunately, they didn't know what life would really be like for them in California.

Chinese miners were not allowed to stake their own claims and could only work claims that non-Asian people had abandoned. They were forced to pay a **Foreign Miners Tax**. In 1882, they were **banned** from **immigrating** to the United States. Chinese miners who left the gold fields found new work washing clothes, digging ditches, and later working on the railroads.

EXPLORE THE WILD WEST!

Did You Know?

Some stone walls, stores, and temples the Chinese miners built are still around today. One example is the Taoist temple in the historic mining town of Weaverville, California. Today, the Weaverville Joss House is a State Historic Park.

WORDS ⭐ to KNOW!

hydraulic mining: using jets of water to move rocks and earth.

debris: scattered pieces of something wrecked or destroyed.

Miners also searched for gold in "dry diggings." They were called dry because miners picked through the soil looking for grains of gold without the help of water. It was challenging to get gold out of dirt. This problem was solved with **hydraulic mining**, which used high-powered water cannons.

While it was a good way to find gold, hydraulic mining washed away hillsides and damaged the environment. It sent **debris** into streams and triggered flooding. Hydraulic mining was banned in 1884. By the end of the 1850s, lone miners were replaced by big mining companies using machines.

MAKE YOUR OWN
Panning for Gold

Pans, picks, and shovels were the tools miners first used during the Gold Rush. In this activity, you are going to compete with your friends to see who can find the most gold. Save the nuggets you mine to use in a later activity.

SUPPLIES

3 miners (players)
gold waterproof paint
paint brush
tiny and small pebbles
pail
play sand
3 plastic tubs
3 tin foil pans
3 forks
timer
3 tweezers

1 Have each player paint 10 to 15 pebbles with the gold paint. Let them dry.

2 Put 1 to 2 pails of play sand in each plastic tub. Add the gold nuggets and fill the tubs halfway with water.

3 Have each player poke holes in their foil pan with a fork to create a sieve.

4 Set the timer for 2 minutes and get ready to dig for gold! Start the timer!

5 Each player scoops up the sandy water and gold with a pan and swirls it gently in a circular motion, letting the sand wash out.

6 Use the tweezers to pick out the gold. See who ends up with the most riches before the timer runs out!

MAKE YOUR OWN
Clipper Ship

The fastest ship in the nineteenth century was the Clipper. The Coleman's California Line advertised that they could reach California in 10 days! Now you can make your own Clipper ship.

1 On three of the sheets of white paper, draw a large triangle and cut it out. On the fourth sheet of paper, cut a triangle about half the size and place it to one side.

2 With a pencil and ruler, divide each of the three large triangles horizontally into four equal pieces and cut along the lines.

3 Cut the top off the smallest piece so that all four pieces are **trapezoids**. Keep each trapezoid set grouped separately.

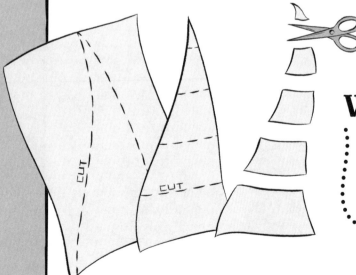

WORDS ⭐ to KNOW!

trapezoid: a shape with four sides. Two of the sides are parallel to each other.

4 Take one set of trapezoid pieces. Punch holes in the top and bottom of each piece in the center. Thread a bamboo skewer through each of the four pieces from largest to smallest to form a set of sails. You can also use the pointy end of the skewer to push through the pieces. Repeat this process two more times. If the pieces are slipping on the skewer, use tape to secure them on the back of the sail. The skewers are your masts.

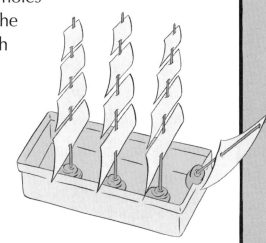

5 Make three balls of clay and place them along the inside of your plastic container. Stick each of the bamboo skewers in a ball of clay to secure them to the inside of the container.

6 Punch a hole in the top and bottom of the triangle piece and poke a bamboo skewer through the holes. Place it at the front of the ship with clay.

7 To recreate the ship's rigging, tie dental floss to the top of each mast and secure it with clay at the back end of the container.

8 Secure a long piece of string to the front of your boat with tape so you can pull your Clipper through the water.

9 Place a few rocks in the bottom of your ship to make it more stable on the water. Your ship is ready to sail! Give it a try in the bathtub or on a pond.

MAKE YOUR OWN
Chinese Lion Dance Mask

During the gold rush many people came from China to California hoping to improve their lives. They brought many traditions with them. The Lion Dance is performed at Chinese New Year to bring good fortune to all.

SUPPLIES

2 paper plates
pencil
scissors
washable paints
colored markers
glitter
white glue
white cotton balls
colored craft pom poms
hole puncher
elastic

1 Draw a semi-circle near the bottom of one of the plates, with the flat line on the bottom. Cut out the semi-circle, leaving the bottom, flat edge attached. Bend this flap down. This will be your lion's tongue.

2 On the same plate, sketch the lion's face with a pencil. When you are happy with your design, go over it with paint, colored markers, and glitter.

3 Make two slits under the eyes with the pointy end of the scissors so that you can see out from your mask.

4 Cut out two ears from your second paper plate and glue them into place. Glue cotton balls and pom poms onto the plate for the lion's mane. Add layers to make the mane thick.

5 Punch a hole near where each ear attaches to the plate. Thread elastic through the holes and tie it so your mask fits snuggly.

MAKE YOUR OWN
Gold Miner's Balance Scale

Balance scales were common in mining town stores because most miners paid for their goods in gold dust. If there was no scale, a pinch of gold dust was worth a dollar! **This project uses a wire cutter and pliers, so ask an adult for help.**

SUPPLIES

2 wire hangers
wire cutters
needle nose pliers
tissue box
colored tissue paper
glue
scissors
tape
string
2 plastic lids

1 Ask an adult to cut the hook off both hangers with the wire cutters. Using pliers, bend one hanger to form three sides of a long rectangle. Make a notch in the middle of the short end where the arms of the scale will balance.

2 Glue tissue paper to decorate your box. Turn the tissue box upside down and poke the ends of the wire into the box. Secure them with tape.

3 Straighten the other hanger and bend it slightly in the middle. Also bend the tip of each end up to prevent slipping. This will be your scale's arm. Place the bend of the arm into the notch of the rectangle and secure the arm with string.

4 Tape four pieces of string to each of the plastic lids as shown. Tie the strings together at the top. Slide the strings over the bend of wire at each end of the scale's arm.

5 Weigh the gold nuggets you and your friends mined in an earlier activity. Did the person with the most gold nuggets end up with the most weight?

Moving West

Do you think you could walk all day, every day, for weeks and weeks? That's exactly what children who walked west with their parents had to do. Depending on where people started and how far west they went, the entire journey could be a few hundred miles or as long as 2,000 miles (3,200 kilometers). It could take five months to get to their new home. No wonder they often went through many pairs of shoes!

Newspaper advertisements made the West sound amazing. They encouraged many people in the eastern United States to move. Often these reports did not give a complete picture of the daily hardships of western life.

People went west for many reasons—not just for gold. Some pioneers dreamed of owning their own farm or opening businesses. The **Mormons** went in search of religious freedom. Others moved west for **patriotic** reasons. They believed that it was good for America to settle all of its land.

WORDS ⭐ to KNOW!

Mormon: a religion founded by Joseph Smith in the early 1800s.

patriotic: in support of your own country.

Did You Know?

On a good day, a wagon covered about 25 miles (40 kilometers). But on days of difficult river crossings and mountain paths, the wagon might only travel 1 mile in the entire day.

At this time, Great Britain still controlled parts of what is now the United States. In 1846, the United States and Great Britain agreed that all of Oregon would belong to the United States. Right away, thousands of peopled travelled west on the Oregon Trail.

The Frontier Wagon

Pioneer families moved west by wagon. A pioneer wagon was light and small. It had to be, to make it through narrow mountain passes. The wagon had a waterproof canvas cover. Because its cover reminded people of a ship's sails, they nicknamed the wagon a **prairie schooner**. Some wagon covers had names or **slogans** such as "Oregon or Bust" painted on the side.

WORDS ★ to ★ KNOW!

prairie schooner: a name given to covered wagons.

slogan: a catchy saying like those used in advertisements.

oxen: adult male cows used to pull heavy loads.

Get Packing!

Most pioneers used **oxen** to pull their wagons. At the end of the journey, oxen could be used to plow fields. They were strong enough to pull 2,000 pounds (907 kilograms)!

A wagon carried everything a pioneer needed to begin a new life. Pioneers usually took equipment to repair the wagon, farm tools, seeds for planting, and personal items such as shoes and blankets. They also brought food such as flour, bacon, coffee, and rice. There were no grocery stores if they forgot something! Trading posts along the way sold some food and other items, but everything was expensive and often sold out.

Families often packed too much. Then they had to lighten their loads along the trail so the oxen wouldn't get worn out with too much weight. Without oxen, pioneers would have to carry their belongings! Furniture, like trunks and beds, was the first thing to be left behind. One pioneer woman left her apron and three pieces of bacon! Eventually there was so much garbage along the trails that people didn't need a guide or a map to find their way.

Did You Know?

You can see miles of wagon ruts along the Oregon Trail in places like Guernsey, Wyoming. The wagon wheels created trenches in solid rock, some up to 6 feet deep (2 meters)!

Unless someone was sick or the weather was bad, people walked beside their wagons. This was mainly to save the space in the wagon for food and to make the load lighter for the oxen. Also, the wagons were bouncy and uncomfortable. The good thing about the bouncing was that pioneers used the motion to churn butter!

Wagon Train

Many pioneers began their journey in the frontier town of Independence, Missouri, where they formed wagon trains. Pioneers believed a large group would keep them safe. There would also be many skills in a group that might come in handy on the journey.

A wagon train could be as long as a hundred wagons or more! A captain led the wagon train. The captain could be the oldest man or the man who owned the most wagons. He decided when the group started, stopped for breaks, and how the group would cross a river. A scout, usually a mountain man, helped the captain. He rode ahead of the wagon train to select tent sites and make sure they were going in the right direction.

WORDS to KNOW!

Independence Rock: a dome-like rock in southwestern Wyoming. It was named for a fur trader's Fourth of July celebration in 1830.

Independence Rock

Independence Rock represented the halfway point on the trail. Children and their parents looked forward to carving their names and leaving messages on Independence Rock. It was significant because people needed to reach it by July 4 or risk getting caught in mountain storms farther west. This giant rock rose 128 feet high (39 meters) and to some looked like a beached whale. If you ever visit Independence Rock in Wyoming, you can still see the names of many pioneers and the dates they were there.

Trail Dangers

Pioneers faced many dangers along the trail. Rain washed out roads. Buffalo could frighten cattle, which would make them run and crush the wagons. Leaving too late in the season could trap pioneers in snow on the way.

River crossings were always risky. If the river was shallow enough, they could wade across the currents and rocks with their oxen. Sometimes they turned wagons into boats by taking the wheels off and emptying them. Other times, families built rafts big enough to hold a wagon by cutting down trees and tying them together. At large rivers, former traders and Native Americans ran **toll** bridges and ferries where families could pay to have their belongings floated across.

WORDS to KNOW!

toll: money paid for permission to cross through an area, or over a road or bridge.

THEN & NOW

THEN: Pioneer families spent $500–$1,000 on supplies for their long, western journey.

NOW: People pay about $400 to fly from the East Coast to the West Coast. They get there in six hours.

Mexican-American War

Many Americans believed it was their right to settle the land all the way to the Pacific Ocean, even if Mexicans or Native Americans lived there. This led to the Mexican-American War in 1846. The Republic of Texas became a state in 1845, but Mexico believed that Texas belonged to them. Mexico went to war to get it back. When Mexico lost, it had to give its territories to America for $15 million dollars. That territory includes the present-day states of California, Nevada, and Utah, and parts of New Mexico, Arizona, Colorado, and Wyoming.

Many pioneers were afraid that Native Americans would harm them. They had heard stories of kidnappings or attacks. Fighting did happen, especially after the mid-1800s. But many Native Americans wanted to trade with the pioneers. And many shared their knowledge with the pioneers, such as the best places to cross rivers and where to look for food.

Disease was the biggest danger on the trail. Many pioneers died of smallpox and mumps. Cholera, which comes from drinking polluted water, caused the most deaths on the trail.

Did You Know?

The Donner-Reed wagon train left for California too late in the season. Their wagons and animals were buried under huge drifts of snow during a fall snowstorm. By the time a rescue party reached them, half of the 87 members had died.

The Daily Schedule

After an early breakfast of cornmeal mush, johnnycakes, or cold biscuits, as well as coffee and bacon, the wagons headed out. Each day a different family led the way. Wagon trains took a break called a "nooning" about midday. While the oxen rested, pioneers enjoyed a cold meal of beans or bacon. Children gathered **buffalo chips** or cow manure to use for fuel on the evening campfire.

WORDS ★ to ★ KNOW!

buffalo chip: a bison dropping that could be burned.

pasture: the land that livestock grazes on.

corral: a pen formed by a circle of wagons to keep animals safe.

At mid-afternoon the train would set out again and travel until early evening. Scouts went ahead of the train to find a **pasture** for the oxen and a large flat area for the wagons. When the wagons arrived they were set up in a circle. The circle made a **corral** to keep the oxen inside to graze. Tents were set up and campfires built.

The Pony Express

It was hard for pioneers to communicate with their families back East. They left letters at trading posts and even under rocks along the trail, hoping that wagons going east would take them. In April 1860, the Pony Express began delivering mail from St. Joseph, Missouri, to Sacramento, California, in only 10 days! Riders changed horses every 10 miles (16 kilometers) and after 70 miles (112 kilometers), a new rider took over.

Trail Food

Women learned to bake bread on the trail using **Dutch ovens** over campfires. Cooking was usually done in the evening and leftovers were eaten for breakfast and lunch.

A typical pioneer diet consisted of bacon, ham, rice, dried fruit, bread, coffee, and tea. They also ate wild game like antelope, rabbits, and birds. Some families brought a milking cow with them to

WORDS to KNOW!

Dutch oven: a cast-iron cooking pot with a lid.

provide fresh milk. Pioneers also traded with Native Americans for meat and vegetables. Everyone ate a hard bread called hardtack. Hardtack didn't spoil on the long trip because it had no butter or lard. Pioneers often dipped their hardtack into a hot drink to soften it before trying to bite into it.

"... out in Oregon the pigs are ... round and fat, and already cooked, with knives and forks sticking in them so that you can cut off a slice whenever you are hungry." —**Peter H. Burnett**

Quick Quote Translation: This meant the West was a place where a person could get rich and live well.

Finding fresh water on the trail was not easy. Rain barrels on wagons collected water, but they never had enough. Pioneers had no choice but to drink from creeks and rivers just like their cattle. One woman wrote of sucking on a rag soaked in vinegar when there was no water. Another wrote about straining pond water through the end of a wagon cover!

The Mormon Trail

Brigham Young became the leader of a religious group called the Mormons after their leader, Joseph Smith, was killed in 1844. In 1846, Brigham Young led a group of Mormon pioneers to the Utah Territory where they founded Salt Lake City. Mormons hoped to be able to practice their faith in peace there.

From 1846 to 1869, nearly 70,000 Mormon pioneers made their way to the Great Salt Lake basin. The trail they created, from Illinois to Utah, was 1,300 miles long (2,092 kilometers). It became known as the Mormon Trail.

MAKE YOUR OWN
Wagon Train Board Game

Between 1840 and 1860, 300,000 people used the Oregon Trail.

1 Use a ruler and marker to draw 15 squares on the poster board. Label each square with the following. Leave a couple of spaces blank.

SUPPLIES

ruler
marker
poster board
tokens for each player
dice

- Oregon or Bust!
- Wagon loses a wheel. Miss a turn.
- Trade for salmon.
- Successfully forge a river. Move ahead 1 place.
- Oxen become sick. Go back to start.
- Pick wild huckleberries.
- Trade for leather shoes.
- Wagon stuck in quicksand. Miss a turn.
- Help a fellow pioneer. Move ahead 2 places.
- Find clean water. Roll again.
- Find pasture for oxen.
- Leave furniture by the trail side.
- In the last square write: Oregon City, Arrived!

Try This!

Print out a map from the official Oregon Trail web site at www.nps.gov/oreg/planyourvisit/maps.htm. Count how many states the trail passes through today.

To Play

2 Each player places a token on Oregon or Bust (square #1). Players take turns rolling the dice. The highest roller goes first.

3 Player #1 rolls one die and moves the correct number of spaces. Once there, he or she follows the instructions. If there are no instructions to move, the player remains on the square until his or her next turn.

4 Players take turns rolling one die, moving, and following the instructions. To win, a player must land directly on ARRIVED!

MAKE YOUR OWN
Covered Wagon

Some pioneers painted their wagons bright colors like red or blue. The color depended on which wagon train a pioneer joined. **If you use an X-acto knife, have an adult do the cutting.**

SUPPLIES

½ gallon juice or milk carton

ruler

pen

X-acto knife or scissors

masking tape

brown, red, or blue paint

paint brush

5 straws

small box for the seat, like a jewelry box

3 pipe cleaners

brown paper bag

permanent markers

cardboard

2 small wooden dowels or skewers

1. Use a ruler to mark a line the long way around the middle of the juice or milk container. Cut along the line and keep one half to use for the bottom of your wagon. Cut another rectangle out of the other half of the container. It should be the same width as your wagon and about 2 inches long (5 centimeters). Put it aside for later.

2. Cover the wagon body with a few layers of tape, making sure to overlap each layer. Remember to tape over the cut edges of the wagon to make it look smoother. Paint the outside brown, red, or blue, and let it dry.

3. Cut two straws into three pieces each. Tape each piece of one straw upright and evenly spaced along the inside of one side of the wagon. Leave an inch or two in the front for a seat (2½ to 5 centimeters). If the straws are higher than the sides, just trim them until they are just below the edge. Do the same on the other side.

4. Bend the pipe cleaners to form three hoops and slide them into the pieces of straw to form the frame for your wagon cover.

5 Cut a brown paper bag to use as the wagon's cover. You can wrinkle it up and then spread it out to make it look more like canvas. Decorate your wagon cover if you like. Cover the pipe cleaner hoops with the paper bag and tape it in place from the inside.

6 Use a small cardboard jewelry box or cut out two rectangles of cardboard to make a seat for your wagon. Cover the seat with tape and attach it to the front of the wagon.

7 Tape the extra rectangle that you set aside in step 1 underneath the wagon. It should extend about an inch off the front of the wagon (2½ centimeters). This is going to support your front wheel axle.

8 Cut out four cardboard circles to use for wheels. Draw lines with a black marker for the spokes. Poke a hole through the center of each wheel. To make the wheel axles, cut a straw to the width of the wagon and tape it across the bottom of the extra rectangle. Cut a second straw and do the same about 2 inches from the back of the wagon (5 centimeters). Push a dowel or skewer though each straw.

9 Slide the wheels on the straw and secure the ends with tape so they don't fall off. You can trim the straws if they are sticking out too much. Your wagon is ready to roll!

MAKE YOUR OWN
Hardtack

Pioneers made a biscuit called hardtack. Hardtack was popular because it didn't spoil quickly. **You'll need an adult to help with this cooking project.**

1 Preheat the oven to 400 degrees Fahrenheit (200 degrees Celsius). Pour the flour into a large mixing bowl. Add salt and mix. Make a well in the middle of the flour.

2 Slowly add water and combine the flour and water using a spoon or your hands. Knead the flour and water mixture until it is smooth.

3 Sprinkle some flour on a clean countertop to prevent the dough from sticking to it. Turn the dough onto the floured surface.

4 Place a layer of wax paper over the dough. Roll the dough out with a rolling pin until it is ¼ inch thick (½ centimeter).

5 Use the cookie cutter to cut out shapes and place them onto a baking sheet. Place the baking sheet into the preheated oven for about 30 minutes.

You should notice that the biscuits are very hard. Pioneers dipped them into coffee to soften them. You can try dipping your hardtack biscuits into a glass of milk!

Pioneer Life

When the pioneers arrived at their destination, there was a lot of work to be done. They started by clearing land and building homes. Pioneers living near forests built one-room cabins from logs.

Did You Know?

Daniel Halladay invented a windmill in 1854 to pump water 24 hours a day. Before this invention, pioneers spent hours collecting water from nearby rivers or pumping water by hand.

EXPLORE THE WILD WEST!

In the Southwest, where there was no forest, they built homes with thousands of adobe bricks. Adobe was made by pressing a mixture of water, sand, clay, and straw into a wooden mold. The bricks were dried in the sun.

There were very few trees on the **Plains**, so people who settled there lived in temporary shelters called **dugouts**. These were like caves cut directly into hillsides by scooping out earth. They kept families safe and warm, but one poor

pioneer got a scare when the family cow fell through the roof!

Pioneers built more permanent homes called **soddies** using blocks of **sod** cut right out of the ground. Windows and doors were made from wood that sometimes came from wagons. The roof was a combination of branches, **tarpaper**, and more sod.

FRONTIER

Quick Quote

"I expect you think we live miserable because we are in a sod house but I tell you in all earnest I have never enjoyed myself better . . . every lick we strike is for ourselves and not half for someone else."
—**Mattie V. Oblinger, June 16, 1873**

Quick Quote Translation: Mattie Oblinger rented the land she farmed before moving west, and always dreamed of owning and working her own property.

Newspapers covered walls inside a soddie, and plaster kept the cold out and the dust from blowing in. Thin cotton fabric covered the ceilings. It helped to keep insects, dirt, and mice out of the food. But nothing could prevent mud from leaking in when it rained.

Pioneer Clothing

There was always work to be done on the frontier, so pioneers dressed in simple clothes. Anything fancy they brought along was saved for Sundays and special occasions.

If a family wasn't living close to a trading center, the women made all the clothing. They grew a plant called flax, which they spun into thread and used to make linen cloth.

Did You Know?

In 1871, 1874, and 1875, swarms of grasshoppers devoured half of the crops on the Plains. These swarms covered up to 1,000 miles of the Plains (1,600 kilometers). The grasshoppers didn't just eat the crops, but also boots, clothes, and door frames!

41

EXPLORE THE WILD WEST!

Pioneers also used wool from a sheep's **fleece** to make cloth. No wonder pioneers wore their clothes until they were worn out!

Men and boys wore long trousers held up with suspenders and loose-fitting shirts of wool or cotton. To keep the dirt and sun out of their eyes, men wore felt wool hats in winter and straw hats in summer. To dress up, men wore vests and a small tie called a **cravat**.

Women and girls usually wore simple dresses in dark colors that did not show the dirt. Women over 15 wore long dresses while young girls wore shorter dresses that were easier to play in. They never wore pants and even rode horses in a dress! Because it wasn't considered ladylike to tan, women wore bonnets with wide brims when they went outside. To dress up, they added ruffles and **petticoats** to their dresses.

WORDS ⭐to⭐ KNOW!

moccasin: a soft shoe made from deerskin.

forage: to search for food or other provisions.

Many pioneers preferred to go barefoot. Some traded their high boots with Native Americans for their more comfortable **moccasins**. They saved their store-bought shoes for church or a dance.

Pioneer Food

By the time a pioneer family reached its destination, most of their food was used up or spoiled. One woman tried to clean her butter in lime juice and churn it into fresh milk! Why? Because pioneers only bought food that they could not grow, fish, **forage**, or hunt. And who could blame them? There were no laws to keep shopkeepers from adding strange things into food products. Flour often contained plaster. Yuck!

Did You Know?

In 1847, Henderson Luelling brought the first fruit trees west from Iowa to Oregon by wagon. Three years later, his brother Seth started a fruit tree nursery where he grew the large, black, sweet cherries called Bing cherries. He named this type of cherry after Ah Bing, the Chinese foreman who helped run the nursery. Today, more Bing cherries are grown in the United States than any other type of cherry.

Families gathered wild berries and roots, and hunted animals such as deer, rabbit, and buffalo. Farmers brought seeds with them for the first planting. After that, they saved seeds from their best plants to use the next year.

Schools and Fun

Not every child on the frontier went to school. Parents taught their children practical skills. Boys learned how to plow fields, harvest **crops**, and hunt. Girls learned how to care for children, sew, and cook. Both boys and girls milked cows and tended the vegetable garden.

WORDS ★ to ★ KNOW!

crop: a plant grown for food or other uses.

teacherage: a simple home built for a school teacher.

In the early days of a settlement, there might not be a school. If parents wanted their children to be able to go to school, they had to build one and pay the teacher too! Many parents didn't have money to pay a teacher. So they gave farm goods instead, such as eggs, vegetables, beef from cows, and pork from pigs. The teacher lived with local families or in a **teacherage** attached to or near the schoolhouse.

Frontier schools were very simple. All grades were in the same room with only one teacher. Children learned to read, write, and do math. Spelling contests were big school events. Even parents competed!

Everyone sat on benches. Desks were simple planks of wood. Children didn't do schoolwork on paper. They wrote their lessons on mini chalkboards called slates. Students used a slate rock pencil to write on their slates, which made a terrible squeaking noise.

They couldn't keep their notes like we do as the slate was cleaned after each lesson. Instead, they learned through memorization. A teacher would say something and the students would repeat it out loud again and again until they could remember it.

Did You Know?

Children had to bring their own books from home, such as the Bible. The earliest textbooks were called readers. These collections of stories were used to teach reading.

EEEK!

EXPLORE THE WILD WEST!

For fun, pioneer children made toys from what was around them. They turned corn husks and rags into dolls and whittled twigs into whistles. Just like you, kids loved playing hide-and-seek, hopscotch, jumprope, and baseball. An indoor game a group of children enjoyed that you may know was "Who Has the Button?" One child left the room, and another hid the button behind his or her back. When the child re-entered the room, he or she had three chances to guess who had the button.

Another favorite passtime on the frontier was music. Children and adults enjoyed singing and making music with fiddles, organs, and other instruments.

Did You Know?

Pioneers learned to make things out of almost nothing. Corncobs and salt became toothbrushes and toothpaste, and they made soap from animal fat.

Presenting . . . Laura Ingalls Wilder

Pioneer Laura Ingalls Wilder moved with her family to Wisconsin, Kansas, Minnesota, and South Dakota. When she grew up, she shared stories of her childhood with her daughter. Rose asked her to write her stories down. Laura Ingalls Wilder later published her first books at age 65. She went on to write eight books in the extremely popular *Little House* series, first published in 1931.

MAKE YOUR OWN
THAUMATROPE

The thaumatrope was a popular toy with pioneer children. This toy has a disc with a different picture on each side. The two images look like one when the disc spins.

1 Trace the bottom of the mug onto the cardboard. Cut the circle out with the scissors. Punch a hole on opposite sides of your circle.

2 Draw a picture that will come together when it is spun. You could draw a dog chasing a ball or a fish and a fishbowl. Draw part of your picture on one side and the rest of your picture on the other side.

3 Tie a piece of string or elastic to each hole. Twist the ends and watch your pictures come together!

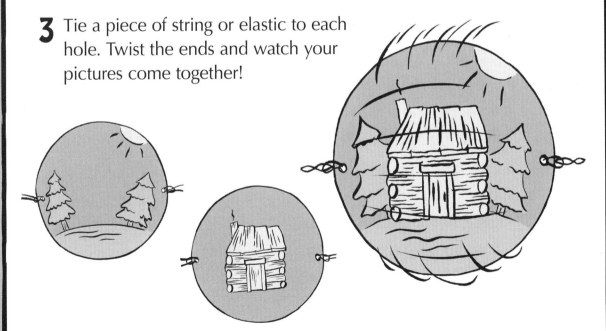

47

MAKE YOUR OWN
Mini Quilt

To keep warm in their chilly homes, pioneers made quilts out of saved fabric scraps. A quilt is made up of shapes cut from fabric that are sewn together. You are going to make a quilt block with nine patches. **This activity requires an iron, so ask an adult to help.**

SUPPLIES

ruler
pencil
white cotton fabric
scissors
freezer paper
iron
crayons
old towel
safety pins
twig

1 Draw a 9-inch square onto the fabric with a pencil (23 centimeters wide by 23 centimeters long). Cut it out with scissors.

2 Ask an adult to iron the fabric to freezer paper to make it more stable.

3 Divide your square into nine even blocks (three down and three across). In each shape, draw a picture with your crayons.

4 Place your quilt design on the ironing board with the drawing facing up. Place an old towel over the block.

5 Ask an adult to plug the iron in at a low setting and press your design. Peel off the freezer paper.

6 Display your block by adding safety pins to the top and threading a twig through the pins to make a hanging rack.

MAKE YOUR OWN Soddie

Many pioneers who settled in the Plains built houses from sod. Sometimes sod was the only building material they could find.

SUPPLIES

margarine container
brown tissue paper
white glue
potting soil
grass seed

1 Take the lid off your clean margarine container and set to one side. Rip the tissue paper into pieces and glue them to your container to form dirt walls.

2 Turn the lid over. Put some potting soil into the base of the lid. Add grass seed and lightly water the soil. Rest the grass seed lid on top of the container.

3 Over the next few weeks, keep the soil moist. Slowly your sod home will sprout a grassy roof.

MAKE YOUR OWN Butter

SUPPLIES

heavy cream
glass jar with a screw lid
dash of salt
crackers or bread

Settlers in the West had to make their own butter from the milk they got each day from cows. In this activity you can try making butter too.

1 Fill your jar halfway with cream. Tighten the lid.

2 Shake the jar until lumps of butter form. This will take a lot of shaking! Say this butter-churning rhyme while you work, "Come, butter come, Johnny's at the gate, waiting for a butter cake."

3 Mix a dash of salt into the butter and spread it on crackers or bread. Store the leftovers in the refrigerator to enjoy later.

Frontier Towns and Lawmen

On the frontier, most people lived on farms. Going to town was an adventure for the entire family. It could take days to get there! Pioneer towns did not have paved roads or concrete sidewalks like we have today. They were simple places where chickens and pigs wandered the main street, which was no more than a dirt track. The trail to town was dusty on dry days and muddy on rainy ones. Mud could become so deep that horses and wagons got stuck! People built wooden sidewalks along the road so they wouldn't have to walk in mud.

Almost all frontier towns had a church, plus a collection of wooden buildings. Pioneers arriving in town headed right to the general store. Nearly anything a person needed could be found at the general store. There were brooms, shoes, gunpowder, medicine, and cloth. Not all pioneers had money to buy goods, so they sold or traded their eggs and crops such as oats and potatoes.

Many buildings had a wooden **false front**. This was a fake second story that rose up above the actual building. False fronts made buildings look larger and more impressive. Some false fronts weren't even hiding a building, but only a tent! And not all frontier buildings were built by the townspeople. Some came in the mail. For $1,000, it was possible to have a schoolhouse shipped west, first in wagons and later by train.

WORDS ⭐to KNOW!

false front: a front wall built to make a building look more impressive.

Many communities in the West thrived and grew into towns. This was especially true if the railroad made the town a stop on its line. Abilene, Kansas, was a town near the railroad that attracted people from the cattle industry. Cowboys brought their cattle to Abilene where they shipped them by train to eastern cities.

WORDS  KNOW!

Transcontinental Railroad: a railroad that spans North America from east to west.

Promontory Summit: the place near Ogden, Utah, where the Central Pacific and Union Pacific railroads connected.

Even more places sprang up once the **Transcontinental Railroad** opened. It connected the East and West Coasts. Amazingly, workers for Union Pacific Railroad coming from the west met up with workers for Central Pacific Railroad coming from the east. They finished the entire line in six years! On May 10, 1869, a golden spike was hammered in at **Promontory Summit**, Utah, to complete the 1,776 miles of track (2,858 kilometers). Suddenly people could travel coast to coast in just eight days!

Did You Know?

The golden spike that was nailed into the last railroad tie connecting the Union Pacific and Central Pacific lines was later replaced with an iron one. The original golden spike is in the Cantor Arts Center at Stanford University in Palo Alto, California.

Eventually, larger western communities formed around an industry like mining or cattle. Bodie, California, was a quiet mining town that started with 20 miners. After gold was discovered there in 1876, Bodie changed into a **boomtown** with 10,000 residents! But like many mining towns, once the minerals were gone, people left and the town busted. Today, Bodie is a Wild West ghost town that is a State Historic Park you can visit.

Famous Lawmen and Women

Many frontier towns had no government, no fire department, and no police officers. This meant that no one was in charge of keeping towns peaceful. **Outlaws**, including cattle thieves and stagecoach robbers, swooped into new towns. Eventually towns hired sheriffs to enforce the laws. In addition to stopping outlaws, a sheriff might round up stray animals, fight fires, or collect taxes.

STAGECOACH MARY: Citizens often had to defend themselves. Mary Fields was a former slave who came west around 1884. At 6 feet tall (2 meters), she dressed in a man's clothes and was armed with a shotgun. Mary delivered mail until she was 70 years old, earning her the nickname "Stagecoach Mary." Mary Fields was only the second woman and the first African American woman to work for the Postal Service.

EXPLORE THE WILD WEST!

WYATT EARP: Dodge City, Kansas, was a dangerous place during the 1800s. Wyatt Earp worked in law enforcement for most of his life. With his good friend Bat Masterson, Earp hid shotguns around town so they knew where to find one in case of an emergency!

Earp fought in one of the most famous gun battles in the West, known as the "Gunfight at the O.K. Corral." Earp, his brothers, and their friend Doc Holliday faced off against cattle and horse thieves and stagecoach robbers. In the 30-second gunfight, three of the outlaws died.

Wyatt Earp is famous for this incident, but most days he tried hard to solve problems without violence. He preferred to knock outlaws out with his revolver rather than kill them.

Did You Know?

In 1852, Allan Pinkerton formed the Pinkerton National Detective Agency. His agency chased down outlaws such as Jesse James and Butch Cassidy. Their logo was a giant eye, which inspired the term "private eye."

THEN: Lawmen learned on the job as they went along.

NOW: Police receive special training at college and police academies.

The Thirteenth Amendment

In 1865, the Thirteenth Amendment ended slavery. But in some states freed slaves still did not have the same rights as other Americans. A man named Benjamin "Pap" Singleton believed African Americans could have a better life. He guided thousands of people to Kansas where they could own their own land.

JAMES BUTLER HICKOK: A legendary sharpshooter, James Butler Hickok worked many jobs, including stagecoach driver, Pony Express rider, Union spy during the Civil War, and scout for the United States army. He was praised for his bravery and skills as a gunman and became known as Wild Bill. After a magazine published **exaggerated** stories of his adventures, Wild Bill became wildly famous!

Wild Bill served as the marshal in several frontier towns. He kept law and order in the busy town of Abilene, Kansas, until he accidentally shot his deputy. After that, he turned in his badge and left the frontier. Like Buffalo Bill, he began performing in **Wild West shows**. He was killed in a card game in the rough town of Deadwood, South Dakota.

WORDS to KNOW!

exaggerate: to make something sound larger, greater, better, or worse than it really is.

Wild West show: a show featuring horseback riding and marksmanship demonstrations.

BASS REEVES: Born into slavery, Bass Reeves was one of the first African American U.S. Deputy Marshals in the West. He worked in **Indian Territory** that later became Oklahoma. In his 30 years on the job, Reeves used his sharp detective skills to capture over 3,000 law breakers.

Bass Reeves was a master of disguise. He would pose as a lady, a cowboy, or a gunslinger to catch an outlaw. He became the first African American named to the National Cowboy Hall of Fame and Heritage Center in Oklahoma City.

WORDS to KNOW!

Indian Territory: land in present-day Oklahoma, where Native Americans were forced to move when their land was taken.

dime novel: a book with a fast-paced story that sold for about 10 cents.

Presenting . . . Buffalo Bill

In the 1870s, Ned Buntline began writing western **dime novels**. The hero of his books, "Buffalo Bill," was based on the real buffalo hunter, Pony Express rider, and U.S. Army scout, William Frederick Cody. The books were hugely popular and Buffalo Bill became a legend. Cody even starred as Buffalo Bill in "Buffalo Bill's Wild West Show and Congress of Rough Riders of the World." In 1899, the show gave 341 performances in 132 places across America! But the show did not always stick to the facts. Native Americans were shown as fierce people who attacked wagon trains night after night, and cowboys were shown as wild men with guns.

MAKE YOUR OWN
SHERIFF'S OFFICE

The sheriff's office is the symbol of law and order in the days of the Wild West. This is one you can eat! **Ask an adult to help as you'll need to use the stove.**

SUPPLIES

Rice Krispies cereal
margarine or butter
bag of marshmallows
large saucepan
wooden spoon
stove
wax paper
can of chocolate icing
black licorice strings
candy star

1 Follow the directions on the cereal box to make Rice Krispie Treats.

2 While the Rice Krispie Treats are still warm, place them on wax paper. Butter your hands and take a small amount of the Rice Krispie Treats and roll it into a log shape. You will need to make about 20 logs. Leave some Rice Krispie Treats unrolled.

3 Spread some icing on a separate piece of wax paper for your base. Now arrange the logs into cabin walls by alternating icing with the logs.

4 Make the roof from the leftover Rice Krispie Treats by pressing it out flat with your fingers. When you have a flat square the size of your sheriff's office, lay the flat piece on top of the cabin walls.

5 Use the licorice to make a door frame and a window. Attach the licorice with icing to the cabin. Place a candy star above the doorway with icing.

6 Now your sheriff's log cabin is a yummy treat ready to serve to friends.

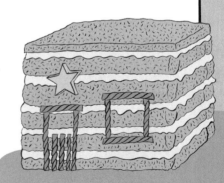

MAKE YOUR OWN
KINETOSCOPE

The kinetoscope was a wooden box used to look at images made on a kinetograph. A kinetograph took many quick pictures in a row. People paid a nickel to look through a slit in the box to see the images in motion. You can make your own kinetoscope and motion picture. **You will need an adult to help you with the X-acto knife.**

SUPPLIES

small box

scissors

X-acto knife

cardboard

paper

2 pencils

ruler

pencil, crayons, or thin-tipped marker

tape

1 Stand your small box up on its side. Make a hole on each side of the box that is big enough for the pencil to fit through. It should be right in the middle of each side.

2 Make a viewing slit on one end of the box with scissors or the X-acto knife.

3 Cut out a circle from the cardboard that will fit vertically inside your small box. Ask an adult to score an X in the center.

4 Cut a strip of paper long enough to fit around the cardboard circle. It should be at least 2 inches wide (5 centimeters), but narrow enough to fit in your box when wrapped around the cardboard wheel.

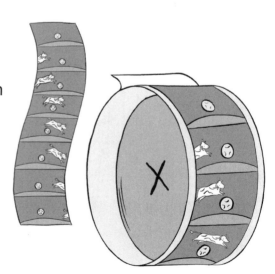

5 With a pencil and ruler, draw lines across the strip in equal segments about every inch (2½ centimeters).

6 On each segment, use the pencil, crayons, or marker to draw a part of your motion picture. Each segment will show a little movement at a time, so plan out your pictures to move along the strip from start to finish.

7 Tape the paper around the outside edge of the cardboard.

8 Push the pencil through one side of the box. Then push the pencil through the scored X in the cardboard wheel and out through the other side of the box.

9 Look through the slit and spin the pencil to see your images move.

Presenting . . . Annie Oakley

Thomas Edison invented the kinetograph and used it to film Annie Oakley. Phoebe Ann Mosey, known onstage as Annie Oakley, amazed audiences by shooting dimes tossed in the air, an apple off her dog's head, and the center out of a playing card. She was so famous, an early speaking movie was made of her in 1935 and a Broadway show called "Annie Get Your Gun" was a huge hit in New York and London.

MAKE YOUR OWN
ℕEWSPAPER

Newspaper and poster advertisements made western towns sound better than they really were. They wanted to encourage people to travel west and settle there. Pioneer newspapers used movable letters on racks to make words. Each letter was placed backwards so that when printed, the word would read the right way. Try making your own advertisement western style. It can be about anything at all that you want to sell!

SUPPLIES

paper and pencil

cardboard

scissors

alphabet pasta

plate

glue

hand mirror

ink pad

unlined paper

1 On a piece of paper, write out what you want to say. Use this as a guide.

2 Cut the cardboard into varying sizes of rectangles and squares for each of your words. The pasta "letters" will fit on these cardboard pieces.

3 Pour the alphabet letters onto a plate. Select your alphabet letters and glue them into words on the cardboard pieces. Remember to put the letters backwards and write the words backwards. Check the words in a mirror to make sure they are correct. Let the glue dry.

4 Holding the first word by the cardboard, push the letters down, onto the ink pad. Press your inked letters onto your paper. Continue doing this until your newspaper is finished.

WILD WEST
NEWSLETTER
EXTRA EXTRA
LOG CABIN
EXPANDED TO
LOG MANSION

LEARN TO PLAY
BUFFALO BILL HORSESHOES

Wild West shows included sharp shooters like Annie Oakley. These men and women tested their skill with a rifle by firing at targets. Test your aim with cookie cutters and a ruler. **Have an adult help you with the scissors.**

1 Wrap your shoebox in wrapping paper and secure with tape.

2 Make a slit in the side of the box with the scissors. Push the ruler into the slit and secure with tape.

3 Stand 4 feet away from the box (just over 1 meter). One by one, toss the cookie cutters, trying to get them to land on the ruler.

4 Make teams and take turns tossing the cookie cutters. You can give more points for cookie cutters that are smaller and harder to toss on the ruler.

Native People in the West

Native Americans lived in the West for thousands of years before the pioneers came. Native Americans respected the land and were thankful for the plants, animals, and natural resources it gave them. At first, Native Americans were curious about the pioneers. They traded furs and their knowledge of the land for horses, weapons, beads, and iron tools. But as more and more pioneers came, Native Americans began to worry about their land and food resources.

Pioneers and Native Americans had different customs and beliefs. Native Americans believed the land belonged to everyone. But pioneers kept coming west and claiming land for themselves. This caused conflict, especially for Native **nations** who lived on the Plains. After the 1850s, war was common.

The Great Plains is a huge area of grassy land in the middle of North America. It lies between the Mississippi River and the Rocky Mountains.

WORDS to KNOW!

nation: a group of Native American people who share a common land, government, and culture.

CANADA

THE GREAT PLAINS

THE ROCKY MOUNTAINS

THE MISSISSIPPI RIVER

THE UNITED STATES OF AMERICA

THE PACIFIC OCEAN

THE ATLANTIC OCEAN

MEXICO

EXPLORE THE WILD WEST!

Before the pioneers moved west, grasses almost 6 feet tall covered the land (2 meters). With its dry climate, few trees, and little water, early explorers called the region the "Great Desert." But the Great Plains is not a desert. It's grassland.

The area was home to the nations of the Plains Indians, including the Blackfoot, Cheyenne, Crow, Comanche, Sioux, and Arapaho. Each nation had its own language, food, clothing, shelter, and way of life.

The Plains was also home to herds of buffalo. The Plains Indians depended on the buffalo for food, clothing, and shelter. Sadly, the buffalo were over-hunted by the pioneers. By the 1880s, the buffalo were nearly wiped out and the way of life of the Plains Indians was gone forever.

Trail of Tears

In 1830, President Andrew Jackson signed a law called the Indian Removal Act. Tens of thousands of Native Americans were forced to leave their homelands and live in Indian Territory. In 1838, members of the Cherokee Nation had to leave their homelands east of the Mississippi River. Imagine more than 15,000 people forced to walk or travel by boat, nearly 1,000 miles from home (1,600 kilometers).

The conditions on the trip were terrible. More than 4,000 men, women, and children died along the way. The journey is known as the Trail of Tears.

From the 1860s through the 1880s, Native Americans fought several battles with the United States Army. These were called the **Indian Wars**. Eventually the Native Americans lost their lands and were forced onto **reservations**.

WORDS ★ to ★ KNOW!

Indian Wars: a series of battles fought between the United States and Native Americans.

reservation: land set aside by the United States government for the Native Americans.

cavalry: soldiers on horseback.

surrender: to give up or give something over to an enemy.

Presenting . . . Crazy Horse

Crazy Horse was a Sioux warrior who believed his people should be able to stay on their land. In 1876, Crazy Horse and Sitting Bull led the Sioux and Cheyenne against the U.S. Army in the Battle of Little Bighorn. They defeated Lieutenant Colonel George Armstrong Custer and his **cavalry**, but were later forced to **surrender** after the army sent in more soldiers.

Crazy Horse is being honored with a sculpture in South Dakota's Black Hills. The monument has been under construction since 1948. When completed it will be 641 feet long and 563 feet tall (195 meters long and 171 meters tall). It may be the world's largest sculpture.

Clothing

Clothing styles and decorations varied among the Plains nations. Women and girls made all the clothing from deer, elk, and buffalo the men hunted. Before animal skins could be turned into clothing, they had to be cleaned and tanned. Tanning was a long process involving scraping the fur off the skin, soaking it, and stretching it on a frame. Tanning made the skin soft enough to use for clothing.

Men and boys wore a **breechcloth** when the weather was warm. Styles were different from tribe to tribe. They wore a decorated **apron** over the breechcloth for special occasions. Leather leggings painted or decorated with fringe and beadwork kept their legs warm. When the weather was cool, men put on **tunics**. Men also painted their bodies with special designs for battles and dances.

WORDS ⭐ to KNOW!

breechcloth: one rectangular piece of deerskin cloth wrapped over a belt and worn between the legs.

apron: two leather panels tied to a belt that hang down in front and back.

tunic: a long shirt.

Women and girls wore sleeveless, ankle-length leather dresses in the summer. In the winter they attached sleeves to the dresses. Many women wore necklaces, earrings, and bracelets of glass beads, metal, and bone. Both men and women wore moccasins on their feet.

Native Americans made their clothes beautiful. Some dresses and men's buffalo robes were painted with pictures that told stories of hunts or battles. Images of horses or buffalo meant good hunting. Clothing was also decorated with natural materials. Porcupine quills dyed different colors, bones, claws, and beadwork arranged into floral or geometric patterns were common.

The men of some nations wore headdresses. The most famous Native American headdress is a warbonnet. These are made from the tail feathers of a golden eagle, and earned for acts of bravery. Warbonnets are impressive, but they were not used by many nations. The most common type of headdress was made from the stiff animal hair of a porcupine, moose, or deer. Woven basket hats were popular west of the Rocky Mountains. Headdresses made with buffalo horns attached and caps made of otter skin were worn on the Plains.

Shelter

The Plains people built housing out of natural materials. Nations on the Northern Plains such as the Mandan or Hidatsa were farmers. They built permanent homes or lodges made from timber, covered with earth and grass. Lodges were circular-shaped homes. The circle had special meaning to the Plains people. It represented life and patterns in nature, such as the four seasons. A fire pit in the center kept the lodge warm. Up to 20 people could live in a lodge along with their best horses!

Plains nations like the Sioux were **nomadic**. They lived in a tent-like **tepee** that could be put up and taken down quickly. Women were in charge of setting up the tepee and they could do it in minutes! They joined poles together at an angle to create a cone shape and stretched a cover of tree bark or buffalo hide over the poles.

WORDS ★ to KNOW!

nomadic: a group of people who move each season in search of food and water.

tepee: also spelled tipi or teepee. A tent-like structure that uses poles and a covering to enclose it.

WORDS to KNOW!

travois: a sled made of two poles, pulled by animals.

Did You Know?

Native Americans used a **travois** to transport tepees. A travois was made from two poles tied together with a net or a platform in the center. First dogs pulled the travois, and later horses.

A small fire built in the center of the tepee provided heat. At the top of the tepee, a hole allowed smoke to escape. A flap worked as a door. The Dakota nation attached ornaments to the flaps that worked like a doorbell. When the ornaments rattled, they knew they had a visitor!

Transportation

For thousands of years, Plains Indians travelled by foot. The arrival of horses changed this. Spanish explorers first brought horses to North America in the 1500s. Native Americans learned how to train these horses in the early 1700s. Horses allowed them to keep up with the buffalo and cover greater distances.

The Nez Perce nation was especially known for their horsemanship skills. They believed horses were gifts from the gods. The Nez Perce rode horses with beautiful spotted coats. Pioneers called the horse the Palouse horse, and later Appaloosa. The word comes from the Palouse River, which ran through the Nez Perce territory.

Another form of transportation used on the Plains was the bull boat. This small circular boat was made of willow branches with buffalo hides stretched over it. Using wooden paddles, Native Americans hauled wood and meat short distances on these tippy boats.

What's for Dinner?

The main source of food for the Plains nations was buffalo meat. Native Americans used every part of the buffalo, not only for food, but also for clothing and shelter. What they couldn't eat right away, they dried in the sun or over a fire and used later. A common food called **pemmican** was made from cakes of dried buffalo meat, berries, and animal fat. Pemmican was popular because it was easy to carry and could keep for years.

WORDS to KNOW!

pemmican: a paste of dried and pounded meat mixed with melted fat and other ingredients.

Plains nations who lived in one location were able to farm. They planted corn, squash, beans, and pumpkins. They also gathered wild fruit such as berries, grapes, and prickly pears. Nomadic nations and farming villages often traded meat and vegetables with each other.

Children's Games

Plains people came together for storytelling, festivals, music, and dance. This is how children learned about their nation's traditions and history. Young girls had dolls and toy tepees. Both girls and boys enjoyed foot races, string games, and ball games. Shinny was a popular game using curved wooden sticks and a ball. Children divided into two teams, and tried to hit the ball into the other team's goal. Sounds a lot like hockey, doesn't it?

Games like "Keeper of the Fire" taught children hunting and gathering skills. To play, a person placed three items representing firewood in front of the fire keeper, who was seated and blindfolded. The rest of the kids were wood gatherers. Their job was to steal the wood without being tagged.

Hand Language

The Plains people used hand signals to communicate with other nations. This was because they spoke different languages. Today some of these symbols are used in American Sign Language for the hearing impaired.

MAKE YOUR OWN
BANDOLIER BAG

Native American women made elaborate beadwork bags for men, called bandoliers. They were mostly used just for fashion and not for any purpose. Before making this craft, look online or in books for images of bandolier bags. **Ask an adult to supervise your online research.**

SUPPLIES

Internet
felt
scissors
tiny beads
fabric glue
fine-tipped markers
safety pins
yarn

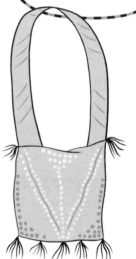

1 Cut out two pieces of felt, each 5 by 8 inches (13 by 20 centimeters). Set this to one side.

2 Cut out your strap. It should be 1 inch wide (2.5 centimeters). The length should be as long as you need it to be to wear it either from the shoulder or across your body.

3 Decorate the front of your bag and strap using tiny beads and glue. Or make a design using fine-tipped markers. You can also glue yarn fringe to the edges.

4 When your beads have dried, use fabric glue to close the sides of the bag. Remember to leave the top open! Attach the strap with safety pins.

THEN & NOW

THEN: Native Americans used a buffalo's hip bone as a paintbrush.

NOW: Native Americans still use natural materials to create artwork, together with modern tools.

LEARN TO PLAY
THE PATTERN GAME

Native American children often played games that helped them become better hunters and gatherers. This pattern game helped them develop their skill of observation.

SUPPLIES

3 players
assorted buttons
dishtowel

1 Choose one player to be "it." This person makes a pattern using some of the buttons.

2 The other players look at the pattern for a chosen amount of time, then cover the pattern with the dishtowel.

3 Each player has a chance to recreate the pattern with the extra buttons.

4 The person who correctly makes the pattern first becomes "it" and makes the next pattern.

MAKE YOUR OWN
Horse Dance Stick

The Horse Dance Stick is a central object in the Sacred Horse Dance. This dance is still performed among the Sioux today. The carved stick looks like a real horse and is painted with red and yellow earth paints.

1 Notch the top of your long tube so that the shorter tube can rest in it. This will make your horse's head. Secure the head to the body with tape.

2 Paint your horse's face and body with paint. Be creative and have some fun! Let it dry.

3 From the paper cut out two ears and attach them to the horse with glue. Let it dry.

4 Add raffia, feathers, and yarn for the mane. When you are happy with your creation, find out about the Sacred Horse Dance of the Sioux.

Did You Know?

Pioneers pressured the government in the early 1800s for more land in the South. But Native Americans already occupied this land. In 1830, President Andrew Jackson approved the Indian Removal Act, forcing nations east of the Mississippi to move to western lands.

Cowboys

Can you imagine what millions of cattle look like—and smell like? Beginning in the 1860s, the West experienced a cattle boom. By the 1880s, there were roughly 5 million longhorns roaming Texas! These are a type of cattle with long horns that come from cattle first brought to America by the Spanish in the 1500s. Ranchers were people who owned large farms for cattle, called ranches. They hired cowboys to take care of the cattle and to move the herds from Texas and other parts of the Southwest to the closest railroad station. Here the cattle would be shipped all over America to be used as beef.

EXPLORE THE WILD WEST!

WORDS to KNOW!

cattle drive: moving a herd of cattle from one place to another.

steer: a male cow that is raised for beef.

But who were the cowboys? They were young men from different backgrounds. Some were Mexican and others Native American. Many were recent immigrants who came from all over the world. There were African American cowboys too, like Nat Love who wrote a book about the life of a cowboy on the frontier. And some cowboys were girls! Women such as Amanda Burks and Elizabeth (Lizzie) Johnson ran their own **cattle drives** and ranches.

It is exciting to think of spending days in a saddle and sleeping under the stars. But there was more to the life of a cowboy. They treated sick cattle, trained horses, and worked up to 16 hours a day. And they were only paid a little over a dollar a day! Because it was too cold to be out with horses in winter, some cowboys also did odd jobs in town to make money all year.

Did You Know?

Ranchers shipped their cattle north because a **steer** worth $4 in Texas could be sold for $40.

Work on the Range

For most of the year, cattle grazed on the **prairie**. In the spring and the fall, cowboys rounded them up. During a **roundup**, cowboys brought all the cattle from their area to one location. All the new calves were **branded** using a heated iron that burned a mark onto their hides. Cowboys also counted and sorted out the steers to get them ready for sale.

WORDS to KNOW!

prairie: the wide, rolling land west of the Mississippi River, that was covered by tall grass.

roundup: the gathering, counting, and branding of cattle.

brand: a mark burned onto a cow's hide by a hot metal tool. The mark shows ownership.

The cattle marked for sale were moved along the trails in spring. That's when the grass was green so they had enough to eat. Who wants to buy a skinny cow?

On cattle drives, cowboys worked in teams of 10 to 15 men called "outfits." An outfit could move about 3,000 cattle. Each cowboy had a task and position, a lot like members of a sports team. The trail boss was in charge of the entire ride. He picked routes and the crew. The straw boss helped him.

Experienced cowboys rode at the front and beside the herd. Newer cowboys worked the back to keep an eye out for stragglers.

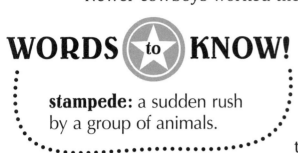

WORDS ⭐ KNOW!

stampede: a sudden rush by a group of animals.

This was the dustiest position. A horse wrangler looked after each cowboy's horses. A cowboy needed to have many horses to finish a day's work because the long hours were too much for one horse to handle.

Dangers of the Job

Cowboys risked drowning when they had to swim cattle and horses across fast-flowing rivers. Snakebites were also a big concern. Cowboys sometimes found a rattlesnake inside their blankets at night trying to keep warm! But the biggest danger for a cowboy was a **stampede**. Lightning, thunder, or certain sights and smells could scare cattle and make them run. To end a stampede, cowboys ran the cattle around and around in a circle until the cattle wore themselves out.

After a long day, cowboys still couldn't settle down for a good night's sleep. They rode around the herd all night to make sure the cattle were calm, switching off every two to four hours. If the cattle were startled, they might stampede. Cowboys also had to watch out for cattle thieves.

Eat Like a Cowboy

The "dough puncher," "grease pot," or "bean wrangler" was one of the most important people on a trail ride. Who was this person? The cook of course! It was his job to feed the crew. The cook prepared meals in a **chuck wagon**. Chuck was cowboy **slang** for food. The chuck wagon carried food and cooking equipment.

A typical cowboy diet was beans, biscuits, bacon, and coffee. If the cook asked you to pass him a couple of **airtights**, he was asking for cans of corn, peaches, or tomatoes. What cowboys really loved were sourdough biscuits. But sourdough had to be kept warm for the dough to rise. How do you think they kept the dough warm when they were outside all night? The cook slept with it!

WORDS  KNOW!

chuck wagon: invented by Charles Goodnight in 1866, the chuck wagon contained food, a stove, medicine, and firewood.

slang: a casual or playful way of talking, like a nickname.

airtight: a canned good.

THEN & NOW

THEN: Cowboys spent months herding cattle along trails.

NOW: Rail transport and trucks take cattle to market.

Cowboy Clothing

Have you ever dressed up as a cowboy? You probably have an idea of what cowboys wore. Most of it had a purpose. Think about what cowboy boots look like. They have a pointy toe and a heel. The pointy toe helped the boot slip easily into a **stirrup** and the heel kept it in place. **Spurs** attached to the heel of each boot helped guide the horse. You could always hear a cowboy coming from the jingle-jangle sound of his spurs!

WORDS KNOW!

stirrup: a loop attached to the saddle to hold the rider's foot.

spur: spikes set on a metal wheel, called a rowel.

chaps: leather leggings without a seat worn over a cowboy's trousers.

A cowboy protected his legs from brush, thorns, and rope burn with **chaps**. Chaps made of goatskin known as woollies were used in the winter. A vest with lots of pockets held a cowboy's tobacco, pocketknife, and other personal objects.

Every cowboy had to have a hat. Cowboy hats had a wide brim to block the sun, wind, and rain, and to protect the cowboy's face from getting scratched by the brush. A cowboy wore a red or blue bandana around his neck. They never wore white because it reflected light and could spook the cattle. Bandanas had lots of uses. Cowboys used them to keep dust out of their mouths, as a sling or bandage if they got hurt, and as a facecloth to mop up sweat.

Rodeos and Country Music

Cowboys loved to show off their ranching skills. They competed to see who could stay on the wildest horse the longest or rope a calf the quickest. Over time, these competitions became known as rodeos. Rodeos are still yearly events in some western communities with their own rodeo stars.

Where did today's "country and western" music come from? Cowboys! Some ranches celebrated the beginning and end of a roundup with music and dancing. On the trail, cowboys sang songs to pass the time while they rode along or sat around the campfire.

WORDS ★ to ★ KNOW!

bunkhouse: a building on a ranch where cowboys sleep together in an open room on narrow beds or cots.

Singing had an important purpose. Cowboys sang to the cattle at night to keep them calm, since any noise could send the herd running. Some trail bosses wouldn't even hire cowboys unless they could sing or whistle!

Back at the **bunkhouse**, songs accompanied by fiddles or guitars were a common amusement. But what did these cowboys sing about? Cowboys sang about events or people on the cattle drive, their favorite horse, and cowboy legends.

Presenting . . . Bill M. Pickett

One of the most famous rodeo performers was Willis ("Bill") M. Pickett. This African American rodeo star introduced steer wrestling.
In steer wrestling a rider drops from his horse onto a steer and tries to wrestle it to the ground. Bill brought his act to Canada, South America, and even performed in England for royalty.

The End

Cattle drives came to an end in the late 1880s. Bad winters killed too many cattle and more railroad stations were built closer together. So cattle drives were no longer necessary.

The invention of strong, spiky barbed wire changed life in the West. Before barbed wire, cattle or sheep grazed on open prairies. With cheap and easy-to-use barbed wire, farmers could mark a farm's boundaries. This kept cattle out, and for cowboys, it meant that their herds couldn't find food and water. The West changed from a land of open spaces where cattle roamed freely, to a land of fenced-off farms.

Did You Know?

In 1890, the United States government declared that the frontier no longer existed. By then towns and cities stretched across the continent. Frontier life lived on in books and Wild West shows.

MAKE YOUR OWN
SCULPTURE

From a young age, artist Charles Russell made sculptures of cowboys, Native Americans, and animals using soap, wax, and clay. When he grew up, he lived with the Blackfoot Nation and later worked as a cowboy before becoming a full-time artist. Today, his art is on exhibit at the C.M. Russell Museum in Great Falls, Montana. **Ask an adult to supervise while you are on the Internet.**

SUPPLIES

Internet
brown, air-drying clay
butter knife
toothpicks

1 Warm the clay in your hands to make it easier to work with. Think of an animal that Charles Russell may have sculpted, such as a cow, horse, or a buffalo. Search for examples of Charles's Russell's sculptures on the Internet.

2 Sculpt your clay by firmly shaping the clay with your hands. Use the butter knife and toothpicks to add details such as eyes, fur, or scales. Use extra clay to build up features such as ears.

3 Allow your sculpture to dry before displaying it. Perhaps you can give your sculpture a special name.

Did You Know?

From 1860 to the mid-1880s, cowboys led more than 10 million longhorns along the trails. It took about two to three months for a herd moving 10 to 15 miles a day to reach its destination (16 to 24 kilometers).

MAKE YOUR OWN Spotted Pup

Spotted Pup is a trail version of rice pudding. Chuck wagon cooks often had to replace fresh ingredients in recipes with canned ones. **You'll be using the stove so ask an adult to help.**

1 Place the cooked rice into a large saucepan. Add the can of evaporated milk and put the pan on the stove to simmer.

2 After about 20 minutes, when the rice has absorbed all of the liquid, remove it from the heat.

3 Stir in raisins, add a dash of cinnamon, and your spotted pup is ready to serve.

SUPPLIES

1 cup cooked white rice (250 milliliters)

deep saucepan with lid

1 can evaporated milk (370 milliliters)

can opener

stove

wooden spoon

¼ cup raisins (60 milliliters)

cinnamon

MAKE YOUR OWN Cowboy Hat

Cowboys wore hats to keep the sun, wind, and rain off their faces. And they made great water bowls for their horses.

1 Crumple the bag until the paper is soft. Cut off the bottom half for the top of your hat and keep the rest.

2 Try the hat on. If it is too tall, cut it shorter. If it is too big, fold over the extra paper and staple the fold.

3 From the extra piece of paper bag, cut out a large oval for the sides and brim of your hat. Staple the brim to the top of the hat and cut out the middle.

4 Roll the sides of the brim and fold the center of the top to form a crease. Glue twine around the base.

SUPPLIES

large paper bag

scissors

stapler

twine

glue

MAKE YOUR OWN
Cowboy Chaps

SUPPLIES

large paper bag
scissors
pencil
hole punch
string
white glue
buttons
yarn
crayons

Chaps were made in many different styles. Batwing chaps are still used in rodeos today. They have large side flaps, fringes, and decorative buttons called conchos.

1 Cut off the bottom of a grocery bag. Cut up the center of the bag so that you have one large rectangular piece.

2 Hold the short end of the bag to your waist and ask an adult to cut a slit up the center for the legs.

3 Lay the bag down and draw the wide batwing shape. Cut off the excess paper.

4 With the hole punch make a hole at each end of the waistband. Tie a long piece of string through each hole to make a belt that ties in the back.

5 Make two more holes near the bottom of each leg, one on the right side and one on the left side. Tie a string through each of the four holes.

6 Thread yarn through the buttonholes so it hangs out the front of the button like fringe. Make a pattern with them on the front of your chaps and glue them to the paper.

7 Cut more yarn into short pieces for fringe and glue them down the sides Take your crayons and add more decorations if you wish.

8 Now strap on your batwing chaps by tying the waistband in the back and the yarn near your ankles loosely around each leg.

MAKE YOUR OWN
CATTLE BRAND

Cattle and horses are branded to show ownership. A brand is like a signature. No two brands are the same so that owners can tell their animals apart. Brands use capital letters, numbers, and pictures such as a ladder or a rising sun. Letters are placed alone, connected, upright, upside down, or sideways. Reading a brand is not easy! **If you look on the Internet for ideas for a brand, you need an adult to supervise.**

SUPPLIES

cardboard

scissors

2 self-stick foam sheets

paint

paint brush

paper

fabric paint

T-shirt

1 Look in books or on the Internet for images of brands for inspiration.

2 Cut the cardboard into a rectangle 1 by 3 inches (2½ by 8 centimeters). This size can vary if you want to make a larger or smaller brand.

3 Cut the foam into the letters and shapes you want to use on your brand. Stick them onto your cardboard to form your brand.

4 Brush some paint onto the foam and press your brand on the paper to see how it looks. Once you are happy with your brand, you can wash the old paint off the foam and paint it with fabric paint to put your brand on a T-shirt!

abandon: to leave behind.

airtight: a canned good.

apron: two leather panels tied to a belt that hang down in front and back.

ban: to prevent by law.

boomtown: a town that grows quickly.

brand: a mark burned onto a cow's hide by a hot metal tool. The mark shows ownership.

breechcloth: one rectangular piece of deerskin cloth wrapped over a belt and worn between the legs.

buffalo chip: a bison dropping that could be burned.

bunkhouse: a building on a ranch where cowboys sleep together in an open room on narrow beds or cots.

Cape Horn: the southernmost tip of South America.

cattle drive: moving a herd of cattle from one place to another.

cavalry: soldiers on horseback.

chaps: leather leggings without a seat worn over a cowboy's trousers.

chuck wagon: invented by Charles Goodnight in 1866, the chuck wagon contained food, a stove, medicine, and firewood.

claim: a parcel of land 50 to 100 feet wide (15 to 30 meters). A miner arriving there first could claim a right to search there for gold or other metals.

clipper ship: a fast sailing ship with three masts and square sails.

continent: one of the earth's major land masses.

corral: a pen formed by a circle of wagons to keep animals safe.

cowboy: a person who works on horseback to care for cattle.

cradle: a wooden box used to sift for gold.

cravat: a scarf worn around a man's neck.

crop: a plant grown for food or other uses.

debris: scattered pieces of something wrecked or destroyed.

denim: a sturdy cotton twill fabric, typically blue, used for jeans, overalls, and other clothing.

dime novel: a book with a fast-paced story that sold for about 10 cents.

discrimination: the unfair treatment of a person or a group of people because of who they are.

dugout: a hole dug in the side of a hill for shelter.

Dutch oven: a cast-iron cooking pot with a lid.

exaggerate: to make something sound larger, greater, better, or worse than it really is.

false front: a front wall built to make a building look more impressive.

famine: a severe shortage of food.

fleece: the fine, soft, curly hair that forms the coat of wool of a sheep or similar animal.

forage: to search for food or other provisions.

foreign: from another country.

Foreign Miners Tax: an 1852 tax of $3 a month charged to Chinese miners.

frontier: the edge of what is settled.

handcart: a small wooden cart pushed by hand.

hydraulic mining: using jets of water to move rocks and earth.

immigrate: to come to a new country to live there permanently.

Independence Rock: a dome-like rock in southwestern Wyoming. It was named for a fur trader's Fourth of July celebration in 1830.

Indian Territory: land in present-day Oklahoma, where Native Americans were forced to move when their land was taken.

Indian Wars: a series of battles fought between the United States and Native Americans.

Isthmus of Panama: a narrow strip of land between the Caribbean Sea and the Pacific Ocean in Central America.

Louisiana Purchase: the land west of the Mississippi River bought from France in 1803.

malaria: a disease spread by infected mosquitoes. It is found mainly in the hot areas near the equator.

missionary: a person sent to convert Native Americans to the Christian religion.

moccasin: a soft shoe made from deerskin.

Mormon: a religion founded by Joseph Smith in the early 1800s.

nation: a group of Native American people who share a common land, government, and culture.

Native Americans: the people already living in America before new settlers arrived.

nomadic: a group of people who move each season in search of food and water.

Oregon Trail: a route to Oregon that was very close to Lewis and Clark's route.

outlaw: a person who breaks the law.

oxen: adult male cows used to pull heavy loads.

pasture: the land that livestock grazes on.

patriotic: in support of your own country.

pelt: an animal skin.

pemmican: a paste of dried and pounded meat mixed with melted fat and other ingredients.

petticoat: a loose skirt with ruffles worn under a dress.

pioneer: one of the first to settle in a new land.

Plains: a large flat area of land in the middle of the country.

post: a fort providing supplies to settlers on the trails and to fur traders.

prairie schooner: a name given to covered wagons.

prairie: the wide, rolling land west of the Mississippi River, that was covered by tall grass.

Promontory Summit: the place near Ogden, Utah, where the Central Pacific and Union Pacific railroads connected.

reservation: land set aside by the United States government for the Native Americans.

roundup: the gathering, counting, and branding of cattle.

settlement: a new community where people have not lived before.

slang: a casual or playful way of talking, like a nickname.

slogan: a catchy saying like those used in advertisements.

sluice box: a long box used to separate gold from dirt.

sod: a section of earth with growing grass and roots.

soddie: a house made of sod.

spur: spikes set on a metal wheel, called a rowel.

stampede: a sudden rush by a group of animals.

steer: a male cow that is raised for beef.

stirrup: a loop attached to the saddle to hold the rider's foot.

surrender: to give up or give something over to an enemy.

tarpaper: paper coated with tar to make it almost waterproof.

teacherage: a simple home built for a school teacher.

tepee: also spelled tipi or teepee. A tent-like structure that uses poles and a covering to enclose it.

toll: money paid for permission to cross through an area, or over a road or bridge.

Transcontinental Railroad: a railroad that spans North America from east to west.

trapezoid: a shape with four sides. Two of the sides are parallel to each other.

trapper: someone who traps animals for food or their skins.

travois: a sled made of two poles, pulled by animals.

tunic: a long shirt.

wagon train: a group of pioneers travelling across the country together by wagon.

water route: a way to get somewhere over rivers and lakes.

Wild West show: a show featuring horseback riding and marksmanship demonstrations.

RESOURCES

BOOKS

Bard, Jessica. *Lawmen and Outlaws; The Wild, Wild West*, Scholastic, 2005

Carlson, Laurie. *Westward Ho!: An Activity Guide to the Wild West*, Chicago Review Press, 1996

Dickinson, Rachel. *Great Pioneer Projects You Can Build Yourself,* Nomad Press, 2007.

Harness, Cheryl. *They're Off: The Story of the Pony Express*, Simon & Schuster Children's Publishing, 2002

Harrison, Peter. *Amazing World of The Wild West*, 2010

Hicks, Peter. *You Wouldn't Want to Live in a Wild West Town!* Children's Press, 2002

Kalman, Bobby. *Life on The Trail.* Crabtree Publishing Company, 1999

Kamma, Anna. *If You Were a Pioneer on the Prairie*, Topeka Bindery, 2003

King, David C. *Wild West Days: Discover the Past with Fun Projects, Games, Activities, and Recipes*, Wiley, 1998

Krohn, Katherine E. *Women of the Wild West*, Lerner, 2000

McCarthy, Pat. *Heading West*, Chicago Review Press, 2009

Miller, Jay. *American Indian Families.* Children's Press, 1996.

Murdoch, David Hamilton. *Cowboy.* DK Eyewitness Books, 2000.

Murray, Stuart. *Wild West.* DK Eyewitness Books, 2005

Randolph, Ryan P. *Black Cowboys*, Rosen, 2003

Schlissel, Lillian. *Black Frontiers: A History of African American Heroes in the Old West.* Simon Schuster Books for Young People, 1995

Slatta, Richard W. *Cowboy: The Illustrated History,* Sterling, 2006

Walker, Paul Robert. *True Tales of The Wild West.* National Geographic Children's Books, 2002

Web Sites

California's Untold Stories: Gold Rush, *museumca.org/goldrush/*
Kidinfo: Pioneers and Westward Expansion
www.kidinfo.com/american_history/pioneers.html
PBS: The West, *www.pbs.org/weta/thewest/*
Museums to Visit: *www.nomadpress.net/resources*

INDEX

A

activities
  Bandolier Bag, 72
  Buffalo Bill Horseshoes, 61
  Butter, 49
  Cattle Brand, 86
  Chinese Lion Dance Mask, 22
  Clipper Ship, 20–21
  Covered Wagon, 36–37
  Cowboy Chaps, 85
  Cowboy Hat, 84
  Gold Miner's Balance Scale, 23
  Hardtack, 38
  Horse Dance Stick, 74
  Jefferson Peace Medal, 9
  Kinetoscope, 58–59
  Lewis and Clark's Route, 8
  Mini Quilt, 48
  Newspaper, 60
  Panning for Gold, 19
  Pattern Game, 73
  Sculpture, 83
  Sheriff's Office, 57
  Soddie, 49
  Spotted Pup, 84
  Thaumatrope, 47
  Wagon Train Board Game, 34–35
African Americans, 7, 17, 53, 55, 56, 76, 82
agriculture. *See* farming
animals, 6, 44, 50, 53, 62, 66. *See also* buffalo; cattle; horses; oxen
Annie Oakley, 59, 61

B

Beckwourth, James, 7
boat travel, 5, 8, 13, 14, 20, 29, 70
Brannan, Sam, 11
buffalo, 29, 44, 64, 66, 67, 69, 70
Buffalo Bill, 55, 56
Buntline, Ned, 56
Burks, Amanda, 76

C

cattle, 29, 33, 51, 53, 75–78, 79, 80, 81, 82, 83, 86
Chinese people, 17–18, 22
Clark, William, 5–6, 8, 9
clothing, 15, 41–43, 66–67, 72, 80, 84–85
Cody, William Frederick, 56
cowboys, 51, 56, 75–82, 83, 84–85
Crazy Horse, 65
Custer, George Armstrong, 65

D

dangers, 29–30, 78. *See also* diseases; violence
diseases, 13, 30

E

Earp, Wyatt, 54
Edison, Thomas, 59
education, 11, 44–45, 51
entertainment, 46, 47, 55, 56, 58, 61, 71, 73, 74, 81–82
explorers, 5–7, 8, 9

F

farming, 4, 26, 41, 44, 70. *See also* cattle
Fields, Mary, 53
food and supplies, 11, 12, 14–15, 26–27, 31, 32–33, 38, 43–44, 49, 51, 62, 64, 70, 79, 84
frontier, 4, 82
fur traders, 6–7, 28

G

games and toys, 46, 47, 71, 73
gold rush, 4, 10–18, 53

H

Halladay, Daniel, 39
Hickok, James Butler "Wild Bill," 55
homes and household goods, 14, 27, 39–41, 48–49, 68–69
horses, 7, 32, 42, 50, 62, 67, 68, 69, 74, 76, 78, 86

I

Independence Rock, 28
Indian Removal Act, 64, 74
Indians. *See* Native Americans
Indian Wars, 65

J

Jackson, Andrew, 64, 74
Jefferson, Thomas, 5, 6, 7, 8, 9
Johnson, Elizabeth "Lizzie," 76

L

law enforcement, 53–56
Lewis, Meriwether, 5–6, 8, 9
lifestyle, pioneer, 39–46
Louisiana Purchase, 3, 5
Love, Nat, 76
Luelling, Seth, 43

M

mail delivery, 32, 53
maps, 3, 4, 8, 63
Marshall, John, 10
Mexican-American War, 30
Mexicans, 17, 30, 76
Mormons/Mormon Trail, 25, 33
mountain men, 6–7, 28
music, 46, 71, 81

N

Native Americans, 3, 6, 7, 9, 29, 30, 32, 43, 56, 62–74, 76
newspapers, 11, 25, 41, 60

O

Oregon Trail, 3, 6, 25, 34
oxen, 26–27, 31

P

Pickett, Willis M. "Bill," 82
Pinkerton, Allan, 54
pioneers
    African American, 7, 17, 53, 55, 56, 76, 82
    clothing of, 15, 41–43, 80, 84–85
    dangers for, 29–30
        (see also diseases; violence)

entertainment for, 46, 47, 55, 56, 58, 61, 81–82
farming by, 4, 26, 41, 44
    (see also cattle)
food and supplies for, 11, 12, 14–15, 26–27, 31, 32–33, 38, 43–44, 49, 51, 79, 84
gold mining by, 4, 10–18, 53
homes and household goods of, 14, 27, 39–41, 48–49
lifestyle of, 39–46
Native American interactions with, 29, 30, 32, 43, 63, 64–65, 74
schools and education for, 11, 44–45, 51
towns of, 50–53
travel and transportation of, 1, 5, 7, 8, 11, 12–13, 14, 20, 24–29, 36, 50, 51–52
western migration of, 1, 4, 7, 24–33, 63
plants, 6, 44, 62, 64, 70.
    See also farming
Pony Express, 32
Porter, Rufus, 11
posts, 7, 26, 32

R

railroads, 51–52
Reeves, Bass, 56
rodeos, 81–82
Russell, Charles, 83

S

Sacagawea, 6
schools, 11, 44–45, 51

sheriffs, 53–56
ship and boat travel, 5, 8, 13, 14, 20, 29, 70
Singleton, Benjamin "Pap," 55
Sitting Bull, 65
Stagecoach Mary, 53
Strauss, Levi, 15

T

tents and tent towns, 12, 14–15, 31, 51, 68
towns, 50–53
trading posts, 7, 26, 32
Trail of Tears, 64–65
travel and transportation, 1, 5, 7, 8, 11, 12–13, 14, 20, 24–29, 36, 50, 51–52, 69–70

V

violence, 17, 30, 53–56, 63, 64–65

W

wagons and wagon trains, 1, 7, 11, 25, 26–29, 36, 50, 79
Wakefield, Lucy Stoddard, 15
water
    drinking, 30, 33, 39
    gold mining using, 16, 18
    travel by, 5, 8, 13, 14, 20, 29, 70
weather and storms, 28, 29, 30
Wilder, Laura Ingalls, 46
Wild West shows, 55, 56, 61, 82

Y

Young, Brigham, 33